Bible Proverbs

Wisdom for Daily Life

Bible Proverbs
Wisdom for Daily Life

Edited by Jude Patterson

BARNES
&NOBLE
BOOKS

NEW YORK

The quotes in this book have been drawn from the
King James Version of the Bible and are assumed
to be accurate as quoted.

2004 Barnes & Noble Books

ISBN 0-7607-6327-5

Printed and bound in the United States of America

04 05 06 07 08 HC 9 8 7 6 5 4 3 2 1

Wisdom is before him that hath understanding;
but the eyes of a fool are in the ends of the earth.
—PROVERBS 17:24

Introduction

SINCE 1611, WHEN THE AUTHORIZED KING JAMES
Version was first published, the Holy Bible has stood
as the most widely distributed and quoted book in
history, surpassing even the works of Shakespeare.
Both religious scripture and practical wisdom, the
Bible has not only influenced secular language, literature, art, and music, but has shaped the foundations
of government, law, and etiquette. Much of the Bible's
practical wisdom has become so ingrained in cultural
lore that many of today's readers are no longer aware
of wisdom's biblical roots.

Bible Proverbs: Wisdom for Daily Life brings
together 250 of the wisdom verses found in the word
of God. Many of these verses come from or echo the
Wisdom Literature traditionally ascribed to King
Solomon, especially the books of Proverbs and
Ecclesiastes. How did Solomon get to be so wise?
1 Kings 3:5-15 tells us that God appeared to the

young king in a dream and bade him to ask God for anything. When Solomon asked for knowledge in discerning between good and evil so that he could rule justly, God was so pleased with Solomon's selflessness that he not only gave him "a wise and an understanding heart," but also bestowed a bonus of riches, honor, and long life. Solomon's proverbs are God-given wisdom. They are for all people whose heart's desire is to see beyond the confines of earthly knowledge to find a deeper wisdom that will guide life's daily choices.

The Bible's proverbs and wisdom verses stand as testament to the enduring and eternal truths of practical wisdom sourced in a higher authority. These truths will never lose their relevance.

—*Jude Patterson*

Adversity

Man is born into trouble, as the sparks fly upward.

—Job 5:7

In the day of prosperity be joyful, but in the day of adversity consider: God also hath set the one over against the other.

—Ecclesiastes 7:14

A just man falleth seven times, and riseth up again: but the wicked shall fall into mischief.

—Proverbs 24:16

The wicked is snared by the transgression of his lips: but the just shall come out of trouble.

—Proverbs 12:13

Rejoice not when thine enemy falleth, and let not thine heart be glad when he stumbleth: lest the Lord see it, and it displease him, and he turn away his wrath from him.

—Proverbs 24:17-18

If thou faint in the day of adversity, thy strength is small.

—PROVERBS 24:10

Confidence in an unfaithful man in time of trouble is like a broken tooth, and a foot out of joint.

—PROVERBS 25:19

In returning and rest shall ye be saved; in quietness and in confidence shall be your strength.

—ISAIAH 30:15

If any man's work shall be burned, he shall suffer loss: but he himself shall be saved; yet so as by fire.

—1 CORINTHIANS 3:15

The fining pot is for silver, and the furnace for gold: but the Lord trieth the hearts.

—PROVERBS 17:3

Give us help from trouble: for vain is the help of man.

—PSALM 60:11

If God be for us, who can be against us?

—ROMANS 8:31

Benevolence

Withhold not good from them to whom it is due,
when it is in the power of thine hand to do it.

—PROVERBS 3:27

The righteous considereth the cause of the poor:
but the wicked regardeth not to know it.

—PROVERBS 29:7

Whoso mocketh the poor reproacheth his Maker.

—Proverbs 17:5

Whoso stoppeth his ears at the cry of the poor, he also shall cry himself, but shall not be heard.

—Proverbs 21:13

He that giveth unto the poor shall not lack: but he that hideth his eyes shall have many a curse.

—Proverbs 28:27

He that despiseth his neighbour sinneth: but he that hath mercy on the poor, happy is he.

—Proverbs 14:21

If thine enemy be hungry, give him bread to eat; and if he be thirsty, give him water to drink; for thou shalt heap coals of fire upon his head, and the Lord shall reward thee.

—Proverbs 25:21-22

Remember them that are in bonds, as bound with them; and them which suffer adversity, as being yourselves also in the body.

—Hebrews 13:3

Be not overcome of evil, but overcome evil with good.

—Romans 12:21

Cast thy bread upon the waters: for thou shalt find it after many days.

—ECCLESIASTES 11:1

Give, and it shall be given unto you; good measure, pressed down, and shaken together, and running over, shall men give into your bosom. For with the same measure that ye mete withal it shall be measured to you again.

—LUKE 6:38

Body, Heart, and Soul

The light of the body is the eye: if therefore thine eye be single, thy whole body shall be full of light.

—Matthew 6:22

The light of the eyes rejoiceth the heart.

—Proverbs 15:30

A sound heart is the life of the flesh: but envy the rottenness of the bones.

—Proverbs 14:30

Keep thy heart with all diligence; for out of it are the issues of life.

—Proverbs 4:23

Who hath put wisdom in the inward parts? or who hath given understanding to the heart?

—Job 38:36

The spirit of man is the candle of the Lord, searching all the inward parts of the belly.

—Proverbs 20:27

Stand in awe, and sin not: commune with your own heart upon your bed, and be still.

—PSALM 4:4

A man's heart deviseth his way: but the Lord directeth his steps.

—PROVERBS 16:9

That which is born of the flesh is flesh; and that which is born of the Spirit is spirit.

—JOHN 3:6

The merciful man doeth good to his own soul: but he that is cruel troubleth his own flesh.

—PROVERBS 11:17

The Lord is good unto them that wait for him, to the soul that seeketh him.

—LAMENTATIONS 3:25

In him we live, and move, and have our being; as certain also of your poets have said, for we are also his offspring.

—ACTS 17:28

Character

A good name is to be chosen rather than great riches, and loving favour rather than silver and gold.

—Proverbs 22:1

A good name is better than precious ointment; and the day of death than the day of one's birth.

—Ecclesiastes 7:1

The memory of the just is blessed: but the name of the wicked shall rot.

—PROVERBS 10:7

The integrity of the upright shall guide them: but the perversity of transgressors shall destroy them.

—PROVERBS 11:3

The glory of young men is their strength; and the beauty of old men is the grey head.

—PROVERBS 20:29

The hoary head is a crown of glory.

—PROVERBS 16:31

As a jewel of gold in a swine's snout, so is a fair woman which is without discretion.

—PROVERBS 11:22

Dead flies cause the ointment of the apothecary to send forth a stinking savour: so doth a little folly him that is in reputation for wisdom and honour.

—ECCLESIASTES 10:1

Pride goeth before destruction, and an haughty spirit before a fall.

—PROVERBS 16:18

Before destruction the heart of man is haughty, and before honour is humility.

—PROVERBS 18:12

A man's pride shall bring him low: but honour shall uphold the humble in spirit.

—PROVERBS 29:23

Let me be weighed in an even balance that God may know mine integrity.

—JOB 31:6

Earth Wisdom

There be four things which are little upon the earth, but they are exceeding wise: The ants are a people not strong, yet they prepare their meat in the summer; the conies are but a feeble folk, yet make they their houses in the rocks; the locusts have no king, yet go they forth all of them by bands; the spider taketh hold with her hands, and is in kings' palaces.

—PROVERBS 30:24-28

Go to the ant, thou sluggard; consider her ways, and be wise: which having no guide, overseer, or ruler, provideth her meat in the summer, and gathereth her food in the harvest.

—Proverbs 6:7-8

Behold the fowls of the air: for they sow not, neither do they reap, nor gather into barns; yet your heavenly Father feedeth them. Are ye not much better than they?

—Matthew 6:26

Why take ye thought for raiment? Consider the lilies of the field, how they grow; they toil not, neither do they spin: and yet I say unto you, That even Solomon in all his glory was not arrayed like one of these.

—Matthew 6:28-29

There be three things which are too wonderful for me, yea, four which I know not: the way of an eagle in the air; the way of a serpent upon a rock; the way of a ship in the midst of the sea; and the way of a man with a maid.

—Proverbs 30:18-19

Doth the hawk fly by thy wisdom, and stretch her wings toward the south? Doth the eagle mount up at thy command, and make her nest on high?

—Job 39:26-27

I watch, and am as a sparrow alone upon the house top.

—Psalm 102:7

The foxes have holes, and the birds of the air have nests; but the Son of man hath not where to lay his head.

—Matthew 8:20

Behold, I send you forth as sheep in the midst of wolves: be ye therefore wise as serpents, and harmless as doves.

—Matthew 10:16

Food and Drink

Let us eat and drink; for tomorrow we shall die.

—Isaiah 22:13

Give strong drink unto him that is ready to perish, and wine unto those that be of heavy hearts. Let him drink, and forget his poverty, and remember his misery no more.

—Proverbs 31:6-7

Look not thou upon the wine when it is red, when it giveth his colour in the cup, when it moveth itself aright. At the last it biteth like a serpent, and stingeth like an adder.

—PROVERBS 23:31-32

Who hath woe? who hath sorrow? who hath contentions? who hath babbling? who hath wounds without cause? who hath redness of eyes? They that tarry long at the wine; they that go to seek mixed wine.

—PROVERBS 23:29-30

The drunkard and the glutton shall come to poverty.

—PROVERBS 23:21

The righteous eateth to the satisfaction of his soul: but the belly of the wicked shall want.

—Proverbs 13:25

The full soul loatheth an honeycomb; but to the hungry soul every bitter thing is sweet.

—Proverbs 27:7

Better is a dry morsel, and quietness therewith, than an house full of sacrifices with strife.

—Proverbs 17:1

Better is an handful with quietness, than both the hands full with travail and vexation of spirit.

—Ecclesiastes 4:6

Better is a dinner of herbs where love is, than a stalled ox and hatred therewith.

—PROVERBS 15:17

Stay me with flagons, comfort me with apples: for I am sick of love.

—SONG OF SOLOMON 2:5

That every man should eat and drink, and enjoy the good of all his labour, it is the gift of God.

—ECCLESIASTES 3:13

The profit of the earth is for all: the king himself is served by the field.

—ECCLESIASTES 5:9

Whether therefore ye eat, or drink, or whatsoever ye do, do all to the glory of God.

—1 Corinthians 10:31

Good Manners

Use hospitality one to another without grudging.

—1 Peter 4:9

Into whatsoever house ye enter, first say, Peace be to this house.

—Luke 10:5

Withdraw thy foot from thy neighbour's house; lest he be weary of thee, and so hate thee.

—Proverbs 25:17

Be not forgetful to entertain strangers: for thereby some have entertained angels unawares.

—Hebrews 13:2

Be not deceived: evil communications corrupt good manners.

—1 Corinthians 15:32

Let no corrupt communication proceed out of your mouth, but that which is good to the use of edifying, that it may minister grace unto the hearers.

—Ephesians 4:29

Happiness

We brought nothing into this world, and it is certain we can carry nothing out. And having food and raiment let us be therewith content.

—1 TIMOTHY 6:7-8

Let your conversation be without covetousness; and be content with such things as ye have: for he hath said, I will never leave thee, nor forsake thee.

—HEBREWS 13:5

I have learned, in whatsoever state I am, therewith to be content.

—Philippians 4:11

Happy is the man that findeth wisdom, and the man that getteth understanding.... Her ways are ways of pleasantness, and all her paths are peace.

—Proverbs 3:13, 17

Delight thyself also in the Lord; and he shall give thee the desires of thine heart.

—Psalm 37:4

He that is of a merry heart hath a continual feast.

—Proverbs 15:15

A merry heart maketh a cheerful countenance.

—Proverbs 15:13

The desire accomplished is sweet to the soul.

—Proverbs 13:19

Hope deferred maketh the heart sick.

—Proverbs 13:12

Even in laughter the heart is sorrowful.

—Proverbs 14:13

I said of laughter, It is mad: and of mirth, What
doeth it?

—Ecclesiastes 2:2

Weeping may endure for a night, but joy cometh
in the morning.

—Psalm 30:5

He that goeth forth and weepeth, bearing precious
seed, shall doubtless come again with rejoicing,
bringing his sheaves with him.

—Psalm 126:6

Health

A merry heart doeth good like a medicine.

—Proverbs 17:22

Pleasant words are as an honeycomb, sweet to the soul, and health to the bones.

—Proverbs 16:24

The blueness of a wound cleanseth away evil; so do stripes the inward parts of the belly.

—Proverbs 20:30

By the river upon the bank thereof, on this side and on that side, shall grow all trees for meat, . . . and the leaf thereof for medicine.

—Ezekiel 47:12

Is there no balm in Gilead; is there no physician there?

—Jeremiah 8:22

Physician, heal thyself.

—Luke 4:23

They that be whole need not a physician, but they that are sick.

—MATTHEW 9:12

I will seek that which was lost, and bring again that which was driven away, and will bind up that which was broken, and will strengthen that which was sick: but I will destroy the fat and the strong; I will feed them with judgment.

—EZEKIEL 34:16

Beloved, I wish above all things that thou mayest prosper and be in health, even as thy soul prospereth.

—3 JOHN 1:2

Bodily exercise profiteth little; but godliness is profitable unto all things.

—1 Timothy 4:8

Be not wise in thine own eyes: fear the Lord, and depart from evil. It shall be health to thy navel, and marrow to thy bones.

—Proverbs 3:7–8

Home

Through wisdom is a house builded; and by understanding it is established: and by knowledge shall the chambers be filled with all precious and pleasant riches.

—Proverbs 24:3-4

Thy wife shall be as a fruitful vine by the sides of thine house: thy children like olive plants round about thy table.

—Psalm 128:3

Every wise woman buildeth her house: but the foolish plucketh it down with her hands.

—PROVERBS 14:1

He that troubleth his own house shall inherit the wind.

—PROVERBS 11:29

He that is greedy of gain troubleth his own house; but he that hateth gifts shall live.

—PROVERBS 15:27

There is treasure to be desired and oil in the dwelling of the wise; but a foolish man spendeth it up.

—PROVERBS 21:20

House and riches are the inheritance of fathers: and a prudent wife is from the Lord.

—PROVERBS 19:14

By much slothfulness the building decayeth; and through idleness of the hands the house droppeth through.

—ECCLESIASTES 10:18

It is better to dwell in the corner of the housetop, than with a brawling woman and in a wide house.

—PROVERBS 25:24

It is better to dwell in the wilderness, than with a contentious and an angry woman.

—PROVERBS 21:19

As a bird that wandereth from her nest, so is a man that wandereth from his place.

—Proverbs 27:8

Every house is builded by some man; but he that built all things is God.

—Hebrews 3:4

Labor

Study to be quiet, and to do your own business, and to work with your own hands, . . . that ye may walk honestly toward them that are without, and that ye may have lack of nothing.

—1 THESSALONIANS 4:11–12

The labour of the righteous tendeth to life: the fruit of the wicked is sin.

—PROVERBS 10:16

A man shall be satisfied with good by the fruit of his mouth: and the recompence of a man's hands shall be rendered unto him.

—Proverbs 12:14

He that hath a bountiful eye shall be blessed; for he giveth of his bread to the poor.

—Proverbs 22:9

All the labour of man is for his mouth, and yet the appetite is not filled.

—Ecclesiastes 6:7

Wherefore do ye spend money for that which is not bread? and your labour for that which satisfieth not? hearken diligently unto me, and eat ye that which is good, and let your soul delight itself in fatness.

—Isaiah 55:2

Let him that stole steal no more: but rather let him labour, working with his hands the thing which is good, that he may have to give to him that needeth.

—Ephesians 4:28

Man goeth forth unto his work and to his labour until the evening.

—Psalm 104:23

In the sweat of thy face shalt thou eat bread, till thou return unto the ground; for out of it wast thou taken: for dust thou art, and unto dust shalt thou return.

—Genesis 3:19

Whatsoever thy hand findeth to do, do it with thy might; for there is no work, nor device, nor knowledge, nor wisdom, in the grave, whither thou goest.

—Ecclesiastes 9:10

The sleep of a labouring man is sweet, whether he eat little or much: but the abundance of the rich will not suffer him to sleep.

—Ecclesiastes 5:12

Laziness

As the door turneth upon his hinges, so doth the slothful upon his bed.

—Proverbs 26:14

As vinegar to the teeth, and as smoke to the eyes, so is the sluggard to them that send him.

—Proverbs 10:26

He also that is slothful in his work is brother to
him that is a great waster.

—PROVERBS 18:9

The soul of the sluggard desireth, and hath nothing: but the soul of the diligent shall be made fat.

—PROVERBS 13:4

The desire of the slothful killeth him; for his hands
refuse to labour.

—PROVERBS 21:25

The sluggard will not plow by reason of the cold;
therefore shall he beg in harvest, and have nothing.

—PROVERBS 20:4

The slothful man saith, There is a lion without, I shall be slain in the streets.

—PROVERBS 22:13

Drowsiness shall clothe a man with rags.

—PROVERBS 23:21

Yet a little sleep, a little slumber, a little folding of the hands to sleep: so shall thy poverty come as one that travelleth, and thy want as an armed man.

—PROVERBS 6:10-11

He becometh poor that dealeth with a slack hand: but the hand of the diligent maketh rich.

—PROVERBS 10:4

Love not sleep, lest thou come to poverty; open thine eyes, and thou shalt be satisfied with bread.

—Proverbs 20:13

Money

A feast is made for laughter, and wine maketh merry; but money answereth all things.

—Ecclesiastes 10:19

Every man also to whom God hath given riches and wealth, and hath given him power to eat thereof, and to take his portion, and to rejoice in his labour; this is the gift of God.

—Ecclesiastes 5:19

The love of money is the root of all evil.

—1 Timothy 6:10

Better is little with the fear of the Lord than great treasure and trouble therewith.

—Proverbs 15:16

The rich ruleth over the poor, and the borrower is servant to the lender.

—Proverbs 22:7

He that oppresseth the poor to increase his riches, and he that giveth to the rich, shall surely come to want.

—Proverbs 22:16

A poor man that oppresseth the poor is like a sweeping rain which leaveth no food.

—PROVERBS 28:3

He that hath pity upon the poor lendeth unto the Lord; and that which he hath given will he pay him again.

—PROVERBS 19:17

Exact no more than that which is appointed you.

—LUKE 3:13

A good man leaveth an inheritance to his children's children.

—PROVERBS 13:22

An inheritance may be gotten hastily at the beginning; but the end therefore shall not be blessed.

—PROVERBS 20:21

Be thou diligent to know the state of thy flocks, and look well to thy herds. For riches are not for ever.

—PROVERBS 27:23-24

Wilt thou set thine eyes upon that which is not? for riches certainly make themselves wings; they fly away as an eagle toward heaven.

—PROVERBS 23:5

The rich and poor meet together: the Lord is the maker of them all.

—PROVERBS 22:2

The poor and the deceitful man meet together:
the Lord lighteneth both their eyes.

—PROVERBS 29:13

Parenting

As arrows are in the hand of a mighty man; so are children of the youth. Happy is the man that hath his quiver full of them.

—PSALM 127:4–5

Children's children are the crown of old men; and the glory of children are their fathers.

—PROVERBS 17:6

The just man walketh in his integrity: his children are blessed after him.

—Proverbs 20:7

Even a child is known by his doings, whether his work be pure, and whether it be right.

—Proverbs 20:11

Train up a child in the way he should go: and when he is old, he will not depart from it.

—Proverbs 22:6

The rod and reproof give wisdom: but a child left to himself bringeth his mother to shame.

—Proverbs 29:15

Correct thy son, and he shall give thee rest; yea, he shall give delight unto thy soul.

—PROVERBS 29:17

The father of the righteous shall greatly rejoice: and he that begetteth a wise child shall have joy of him.

—PROVERBS 23:24

Better is a poor and a wise child than an old and foolish king, who will no more be admonished.

—ECCLESIASTES 4:13

He that delicately bringeth up his servant from a child shall have him become his son at the length.

—PROVERBS 29:21

I was my father's son, tender and only beloved in the sight of my mother. He taught me also, and said unto me, Let thine heart retain my words: keep my commandments, and live.

—Proverbs 4:3–4

Relationships

Two are better than one; because they have a good reward for their labour.

—Ecclesiastes 4:9

A man that hath friends must shew himself friendly: and there is a friend that sticketh closer than a brother.

—Proverbs 18:24

A friend loveth at all times, and a brother is born for adversity.

—Proverbs 17:17

A brother offended is harder to be won than a strong city: and their contentions are like the bars of a castle.

—Proverbs 18:19

Faithful are the wounds of a friend; but the kisses of an enemy are deceitful.

—Proverbs 27:6

Deliver thyself, when thou art come into the hand of thy friend; go, humble thyself, and make sure thy friend.

—Proverbs 6:3

The discretion of a man deferreth his anger; and it is his glory to pass over a transgression.

—Proverbs 19:11

Make no friendship with an angry man; and with a furious man thou shalt not go: lest thou learn his ways, and get a snare to thy soul.

—Proverbs 22: 24-25

Thine own friend, and thy father's friend, forsake not; neither go into thy brother's house in the day of thy calamity: for better is a neighbour that is near than a brother far off.

—Proverbs 27:10

If two lie together, then they have heat: but how can one be warm alone?

—ECCLESIASTES 4:11

Who can find a virtuous woman? for her price is far above rubies. The heart of her husband doth safely trust in her, so that he shall have no need of spoil.

—PROVERBS 31:10-11

When a man hath taken a new wife, he shall not go out to war, neither shall he be charged with any business: but he shall be free at home one year, and shall cheer up his wife which he hath taken.

—DEUTERONOMY 24:5

Live joyfully with the wife whom thou lovest all the days of the life of thy vanity.

—ECCLESIASTES 9:9

Responsibility

Whatsoever a man soweth, that shall he also reap.

—GALATIANS 6:7

In the morning sow thy seed, and in the evening withhold not thine hand: for thou knowest not whether shall prosper, either this or that, or whether they both shall be alike good.

—ECCLESIASTES 11:6

He that observeth the wind shall not sow; and he that regardeth the clouds shall not reap.

—ECCLESIASTES 11:4

He which soweth sparingly shall reap also sparingly; and he which soweth bountifully shall reap also bountifully.

—2 CORINTHIANS 9:6

They that sow in tears shall reap in joy.

—PSALM 126:5

They have sown the wind, and they shall reap the whirlwind.

—HOSEA 8:7

He that soweth iniquity shall reap vanity: and the rod of his anger shall fail.

—PROVERBS 22:8

They that plow iniquity, and sow wickedness, reap the same.

—JOB 4:8

Ye have plowed wickedness, ye have reaped iniquity; ye have eaten the fruit of lies: because thou didst trust in thy way, in the multitude of thy mighty men.

—HOSEA 10:13

He that soweth to his flesh shall of the flesh reap corruption; but he that soweth to the Spirit shall of the Spirit reap life everlasting.

—GALATIANS 6:8

The sower soweth the word.

—MARK 4:14

Talk

For he that will love life, and see good days, let him refrain his tongue from evil, and his lips that they speak no guile.

—1 Peter 3:10

Those things which proceed out of the mouth come forth from the heart.

—Matthew 15:18

The heart of the wise teacheth his mouth, and addeth learning to his lips.

—PROVERBS 16:13

Ointment and perfume rejoice the heart: so doth the sweetness of a man's friend by hearty counsel.

—PROVERBS 27:9

Heaviness in the heart of man maketh it stoop: but a good word maketh it glad.

—PROVERBS 12:25

A word fitly spoken is like apples of gold in pictures of silver.

—PROVERBS 25:11

A soft answer turneth away wrath: but grievous words stir up anger.

—Proverbs 15:1

The north wind driveth away rain: so doth an angry countenance a back-biting tongue.

—Proverbs 25:23

Debate thy cause with thy neighbour himself; and discover not a secret to another.

—Proverbs 25:9

A man that beareth false witness against his neighbour is a maul, and a sword, and a sharp arrow.

—Proverbs 25:18

He that goeth about as a talebearer revealeth secrets: therefore meddle not with him that flattereth with his lips.

—Proverbs 20:19

A talebearer revealeth secrets: but he that is of a faithful spirit concealeth the matter.

—Proverbs 11:13

The words of a talebearer are as wounds, and they go down into the innermost parts of the belly.

—Proverbs 26:22

He that covereth a transgression seeketh love; but he that repeateth a matter separateth very friends.

—Proverbs 17:9

Surely the serpent will bite without enchantment; and a babbler is no better.

—Ecclesiastes 10:11

The tongue is a little member, and boasteth great things. Behold, how great a matter a little fire kindleth!

—James 3:5

Whoso boasteth himself of a false gift is like clouds and wind without rain.

—Proverbs 25:14

Let another man praise thee, and not thine own mouth; a stranger, and not thine own lips.

—Proverbs 27:2

He that hath knowledge spareth his words: and a man of understanding is of an excellent spirit. Even a fool, when he holdeth his peace, is counted wise: and he that shutteth his lips is esteemed a man of understanding.

—Proverbs 17:27-28

Be not rash with thy mouth, and let not thine heart be hasty to utter anything before God: for God is in heaven, and thou upon earth: therefore let thy words be few.

—Ecclesiastes 5:2

Let your speech be alway with grace, seasoned with salt, that ye may know how ye ought to answer every man.

—Colossians 4:6

Take no heed unto all words that are spoken; lest thou hear thy servant curse thee: for oftentimes also thine own heart knoweth that thou thyself likewise hast cursed others.

—ECCLESIASTES 7:21-22

Death and life are in the power of the tongue: and they that love it shall eat the fruit thereof.

—PROVERBS 18:21

If thou hast done foolishly in lifting up thyself, or if thou hast thought evil, lay thine hand upon thy mouth.

—PROVERBS 30:32

Thoughts

Curse not the king, no not in thy thought; and curse not the rich in thy bedchamber: for a bird of the air shall carry the voice, and that which hath wings shall tell the matter.

—ECCLESIASTES 10:20

The thoughts of the righteous are right: but the counsels of the wicked are deceit.

—PROVERBS 12:5

The thoughts of the diligent tend only to plenteousness; but of every one that is hasty only to want.

—PROVERBS 21:5

If a man think himself to be something, when he is nothing, he deceiveth himself.

—GALATIANS 6:3

The spirit of man is the candle of the Lord, searching all the inward parts of the belly.

—PROVERBS 20:27

Whatsoever things are true, whatsoever things are honest, whatsoever things are just, whatsoever things are pure, whatsoever things are lovely, whatsoever things are of good report; if there be any virtue, and if there be any praise, think on these things.

—Philippians 4:10

Commit thy works unto the Lord, and thy thoughts shall be established.

—Proverbs 16:3

In the multitude of thy thoughts within me thy comforts delight my soul.

—Psalm 94:19

Let the words of my mouth, and the meditation of my heart, be acceptable in thy sight, O Lord, my strength and my redeemer.

—PSALM 19:14

Tomorrow

Who knoweth what is good for man in this life,
all the days of his vain life which he spendeth as
a shadow? for who can tell a man what shall be
after him under the sun?

—ECCLESIASTES 6:12

Boast not thyself of to morrow; for thou knowest
not what a day may bring forth.

—PROVERBS 27:1

Ye know not what shall be on the morrow. For what is your life? It is even a vapour, that appeareth for a little time, and then vanisheth away.

—JAMES 4:14

The days of our years are threescore years and ten; and if by reason of strength they be fourscore years, yet is their strength labour and sorrow; for it is soon cut off, and we fly away.

—PSALM 90:10

One generation passeth away, and another generation cometh: but the earth abideth for ever. The sun also ariseth, and the sun goeth down, and hasteth to his place where he arose.

—ECCLESIASTES 1:4-5

The thing that hath been, it is that which shall be; and that which is done is that which shall be done: and there is no new thing under the sun.

—Ecclesiastes 1:9

All things have I seen in the days of my vanity: there is a just man that perisheth in his righteousness, and there is a wicked man that prolongeth his life in his wickedness.... Lo, this only have I found, that God hath made man upright; but they have sought out many inventions.

—Ecclesiates 7:15, 29

The race is not to the swift, nor the battle to the strong, neither yet bread to the wise, nor yet riches to men of understanding, nor yet favour to men of skill; but time and chance happeneth to them all.

—Ecclesiastes 9:11

There is no remembrance of the wise more than of the fool for ever; seeing that which now is in the days to come shall all be forgotten. And how dieth the wise man? as the fool.

—ECCLESIASTES 2:17

Take no thought for the morrow: for the morrow shall take thought for the things of itself. Sufficient unto the day is the evil thereof.

—MATTHEW 7:34

Teach us to number our days, that we may apply our hearts unto wisdom.

—PSALM 90:12

Wisdom

Wisdom is a defence, and money is a defence: but the excellency of knowledge is, that wisdom giveth life to them that have it.

—ECCLESIASTES 7:12

When wisdom entereth into thine heart, and knowledge is pleasant unto thy soul; discretion shall preserve thee, understanding shall keep thee.

—PROVERBS 2:10-11

Wisdom is the principal thing; therefore get wisdom: and with all thy getting get understanding.

—Proverbs 4:7

Wisdom is before him that hath understanding; but the eyes of a fool are in the ends of the earth.

—Proverbs 17:24

A fool hath no delight in understanding, but that his heart may discover itself.

—Proverbs 18:2

In much wisdom is much grief: and he that increaseth knowledge increaseth sorrow.

—Ecclesiastes 1:18

With the ancient is wisdom; and in length of days understanding.

—JOB 12:12

Who is the wise man? and who knoweth the interpretation of a thing? a man's wisdom maketh his face to shine, and the boldness of his face shall be changed.

—ECCLESIASTES 8:1

Knowledge puffeth up, but charity edifieth. If any man think that he knoweth any thing, he knoweth nothing yet as he ought to know.

—1 CORINTHIANS 8:1-2

Let no man deceive himself. If any man among you seemeth to be wise in this world, let him become a fool, that he may be wise.

—1 CORINTHIANS 3:18

It is the glory of God to conceal a thing: but the honour of kings is to search out a matter.

—PROVERBS 25:2

The queen of the south shall rise up in the judgment with the men of this generation, and condemn them: for she came from the utmost parts of the earth to hear the wisdom of Solomon; and, behold, a greater than Solomon is here.

—LUKE 11:31

Word of God

It is written, Man shall not live by bread alone, but by every word that proceedeth out of the mouth of God.

—MATTHEW 4:4

All scripture is given by inspiration of God, and is profitable for doctrine, for reproof, for correction, for instruction in righteousness: that the man of God may be perfect, thoroughly furnished unto all good works.

—2 TIMOTHY 3:16-17

Every word of God is pure: he is a shield unto them that put their trust in him.

—PROVERBS 30:5

The word of God is quick, and powerful, and sharper than any two-edged sword, piercing even to the dividing asunder of soul and spirit, and of the joints and marrow, and is a discerner of the thoughts and intents of the heart.

—HEBREWS 4:12

Take the helmet of salvation, and the sword of the Spirit, which is the word of God.

—EPHESIANS 6:17

These words, which I command thee this day, shall be in thine heart: And thou shalt teach them diligently unto thy children, and shalt talk of them when thou sittest in thine house, and when thou walkest by the way, and when thou liest down, and when thou risest up.

—Deuteronomy 6:6-7

This book of the law shall not depart out of thy mouth; but thou shalt meditate therein day and night, that thou mayest observe to do according to all that is written therein: for then thou shalt make thy way prosperous, and then thou shalt have good success.

—Joshua 1:8

Let us hear the conclusion of the whole matter: Fear God, and keep his commandments: for this is the whole duty of man.

—ECCLESIASTES 12:13

All the law is fulfilled in one word, even in this; Thou shalt love thy neighbour as thyself.

—GALATIANS 5:14

I have set before thee an open door, and no man can shut it: for thou hast a little strength, and hast kept my word, and hast not denied my name.

—REVELATION 3:8

Behold, I stand at the door, and knock: if any man hear my voice, and open the door, I will come in to him, and will sup with him, and he with me.

—REVELATION 3:20